Unmasking The Christian

Amanda Sekati

ISBN 978-93-5610-923-0

Published in India 2022 by Pencil

Contributors:
Editor: Tsholofelo Divine Dhlomo
Editor: Ivy

A brand of
One Point Six Technologies Pvt. Ltd.
123, Building J2, Shram Seva Premises,
Wadala Truck Terminal, Wadala (E)
Mumbai 400037, Maharashtra, INDIA
E connect@thepencilapp.com
W www.thepencilapp.com

Author biography

Amanda Sekati, author of Unmasking The Christian

Amanda Sekati was born and raised in the City of Johannesburg, aside from New York, that's the other city that never sleeps in the beautiful country South Africa. Amanda considers her faith in Christ and family to be most important to her. If she isn't spending time with her friends and family, you can almost always find her in a quiet space or making glamorous garments. Unmasking the Christian is Amanda's first book.

Note: Amanda Sekati paints a picture of a person who had to walk the journey of a Christian and still handle growing up in "real world". This gives the reader a comforting sense that the writer is understanding and had to learn to heal, unlearn traits and find her way back to herself after life "showed her flames". Unmasking the Christian

CONTENTS

Epigraph

UNMASKING THE CHRISTIAN

First printing 2022
Printed in South Africa

Introduction

Unmasking the Christian

This book simply was written as a testimony of my life and giving Glory to the great Lord for times I didn't even acknowledge Him.

In the year 2018 I went through the most depressing time of my life and while in seek of finding the lost pieces to build myself again, I reflected on the word of God.

I searched myself in Him and through Him but before He could rebuild me again, He had to take me apart and remove all the damaged pieces to restore me with new ones. In order to change I had to confront my fears, habits, and hidden scars.

Isaiah 43:7

Everyone who is called by my name,
Whom I created for my glory,
Whom, I formed and made.

While being broken into pieces He reminded me of all I have been through and how present He was.

Deuteronomy 31:6

"Be strong and courageous. Do not be afraid or terrified because of them, for the LORD your God goes with you; he will never leave you or forsake you"

He was there with me, always, and wanted me to share these testimonies.

Every morning started with new mercies and glory.

Chapter One- Unlayer

In May 2018, I decided to dedicate myself to getting to know God better. For the longest time, I have been comfortable being the average Christian, the one who goes to church every Sunday, prays before she eats, and attends all church programs. I pretty much thought I was the ultimate church girl, friends from church and even dated strictly from the church but then I had an awakening.

Matthew 6:33 says ***"But seek first the kingdom of God and His righteousness, and all these things will be added unto you.*** "And I did everything and even claimed my Christianity but never actually searched for the Lord and His word.

So, I committed myself to a message a day, a scripture or bible plan, and gospel music. I know, I thought that was boring too, but listen for a minute. Seeking God was not in just the actions I took but, in the willingness, to do them. We all know God trusts our hearts more than actions because actions can be done out of malicious intentions, pride, the pressure of what people will say, and the fear of going to hell, whatever your reason may be, but what God wants is the purity of your heart, if your heart seeks Him first it becomes easier to do according to your hearts desires. ***Proverbs 27:19 "As in water face reflects face, so the heart of man reflects the man."*** So, what our

hearts want, and feel is what will reflect on the outside.
I then tried harder to spend time listening to the word of God. I would mostly dedicate my morning train trip to work because it was easier with no distractions and conversations happening around me. It was a convenient time because my friends were not around, and I didn't have to get into the latest gossip. This was going well, I had a favorite message I would listen to from the Fruitfulness series from Transformation church, and the message was Peace under Pressure. I listened to it all the time, not knowing God was preparing me for a wave that was coming for me.

In August 2018, the wave came rushing in like a July winter breeze. I lost my job, my business wasn't succeeding as I had planned, I had a fall out with one of my mentors and my relationship wasn't making much sense at the time. Everything I had depended on as comfort had finally left me with no crutch to stand on. At the age of 25, I expected to be doing at least "alright" instead, I felt hopeless, lost, out of place, and confused about my next steps, because you see just because my life was a mess, didn't mean I didn't have people depending on me to still stand on my two feet and get things done.
I had to push here and there, but still battling with emotions and mental and financial breakdowns. At this point, I had nowhere else to turn but the word, I dedicated myself fully, to prayer, studying, and meditating on Peace Under Pressure. But you see to find peace in its fullness, you not only need to find God and His kind of peace but must find the things that cause discomfort and pressure and tear them down.

This is the journey God took me through, that not only was He present during the pressures of life, but He'd help me lose the weight of burdens I didn't know I had been carrying. I had to relive moments that shaped the way I think and do life, and boooy was I never ready.

Chapter Two- Great Loss

Losing a loved one can be very painful, and for some people life-changing, I was only 14 years old, when my father passed on. I cannot begin to describe the feeling I felt. It was like my world had come to an end. I remember running out of the house with no specific destination, but I needed to breathe different air. I was suffocating and drowning in tears all at the same time.

Through this journey of discovery< God wanted me to relive these emotions all over again, cry and remember the feeling of struggling to breathe, sleep, eat and function normally.

I remember the feeling I felt every time people would mention my father or reference him, it would hit me all over again that he's no longer around. I became a loner from then on, always angry, furious that he left so early in my life, I was furious with God for taking him, I was mad at myself. I had anger, and rage and I needed an outlet, something to numb my pain or at least distract me from reality.

It was a great loss for me, my best friend had left me because you see, I was loved and I knew it. I had a love like no other and my father gave it on overload. I didn't have to seek love from anywhere else because the one person I needed it from, gave it to me. He was my best friend, hero, and everything I needed a father to be, he made me feel blessed and "lucky", untouchable, and like a princess. But now I had lost that, that security in a man. That stability and love that only a father as great as he, can provide, no more walks in the park, random drives to Pretoria without my mother's knowledge, spontaneous ice cream and bunny chow trips, catching up on DragonballZ, no one to serve me that first cup of Milo in bed before the day started. Yes, I was spoiled and treated like royalty. Everything that had been comforting and a safe place for me was taken from me in a blink and there was no way of getting it back. He was gone, to a place I can never reach him.

Acceptance was my next step, because for a long time as well, all I wanted was to forget about it, but every time I was reminded of his death, it would hit me like a brick to the face. I remember finding ways to distract myself, ways to mute the pain, ease the hurt and possibly make everyone around me forget. I hated being pitied, the "I am sorry for your loss" began to bother me, and I needed everyone to forget that I was in pain. Pain, is a powerful emotion, something you cannot really run away from, part of the human cycle. And my Christianity was not as strong then as it is now, so I went my own ways. I spent time making friends and figuring out interests in music and things to entertain myself and others. I had something else to talk about other than the loss of my father. I had to find ways out. I found myself going to church more and more, not to learn about God and His Word, but it was all I knew. It was a familiar place where my life had always happened, and so there must have been something there for me. Is not it funny how we do not recognize God working even when He is? He took me to the one place most people would not go, instead of drugs and outside distractions; He created a place for me in His house for comfort. Anyway, somehow I fell in love with hip-hop and started dancing, in church, that was my outlet from the pain and hurt for a very long time.

Psalm 68, verse 5: "A Father to the fatherless..." I understand that scripture now. He did not have to be physical to make me whole again; I just needed to be available and willing to hear. But as a teenager, we believe more in the physical than the spiritual, friends and family provide for us and make things happen, so even though I found dancing in church I still had a huge hole to fill. I still needed a distraction, something to get my mind off my father's death. Seeking anything to help me forget, sounds like a drug right… well...

Chapter Three- Self Medicating

I found a way to help ease my pain, to help me forget, or at least give me a few hours of happiness without any memory of pain. When in pain a quick fix is all you need, unfortunately, most of them are temporary. My way of escape was dating, I searched for an ounce of love my father gave me in others, seeking the affection he would give me and love with no borders. I also convinced myself that every guy I dated was sent by God, I searched for some Christian element in them, whether they were born again, go to the same church or ministry as I have, any Christian link or lifestyle, or something that pleased me enough to believe that at least they aren't that bad.

Relationships are typically the most common escape for most young people, we find a person to give us attention and for us to give attention to, to give us a different world to live in, where laughter, love, and fairy tale romance exist.

I remember with my first boyfriend, we were introduced by my cousin and spent most of our relationship on social media, Mxit days. He called himself "prince charming", looks I agree, but his character was debatable. If you ask me now, what it was that made me think we could make it, I really have no response. My family has always been Christian, and my father was an evangelist. So, I guess finding a guy interesting would have to have those qualities. His father was a pastor and he loved his mother and little sister, so some family element. His birthday was a day before my father's, and I believed that was the sign that he was "the one", the one to save me from all this pain, misery, and anguish, the one to make me happy again, free again and a princess again. The things we tell ourselves when we think we're in love.

I spent my time obsessing about our relationship and committing myself to a version I thought he was. You see, because that's what we humans do, we fall for fractions of people and expect that fraction to fill up a whole, to fill a void. I have used dating as an escape. Definition of "escape' -a form of a temporary distraction from reality or routine. And that's exactly what I thought I needed. My relationship with prince charming lasted 4 years with a few break-ups and make-ups here and there; it was a cycle of Beyoncé-Ave Maria and Beyoncé's Broken-hearted girl. Our biggest issue was that he was never available, I was okay with a long-distance relationship, but I hoped he would like me enough to want to see me. He and I never really spent real time together, we met in passing and not on purpose, because everything I planned for us was never a good time for him, he was either babysitting or didn't have the car with him, or with his mother, (excuses, excuses).

We called it quits when it wasn't working, then miss each other and decide to begin again. But in between those break-ups I dated a few people as well, yes pretty messed up I know, but every time we broke up, we were sure it was final and never again.

So, I remember meeting this one guy at a church conference, he was gorgeous and had the most gorgeous afro. A bit of goon himself, life of the crowd, cracked jokes and was oddly placed sometimes. I had a thing for guys, people wouldn't typically fall for or gravitate towards, and I guess that should've been my sign because all of them were nothing like what I expected.

Anyways, we had a moment during the conference, where we had to greet each other and so there was an exchange of words and a small conversation. My friend and I found interest in him and decided to name him Afropop. Months later we met again and exchanged numbers, started talking, and were, I guess now dating. With him I felt free to be me, I guess he allowed me to not filter my reality, from my previous relationship, I was introduced to rock music and so I carried that into this relationship, pace with me it's an important detail. He allowed me to have feelings and let my guard down because as my sister would say, I had a barbwire, electric fence, metal and steel gates, concrete walls, pit bulls, and locks around my heart. No one could get in, but I guess I allowed him a bit of access. he allowed himself to be vulnerable as well, he shared pieces of his truth and I think that's what really captured my heart, we also shared the love of Rock music and had a "song" Metric- All Yours, boooy was I smitten, the vulnerability of those lyrics took me by surprise and had me head over hills in days, but like Taraji P Henson said in Acrimony "The devil sure knows how to put a package together."

A few days later of "dating", I was invited to his 18th birthday party, no big deal right, I'll go with my bestie and spend some time with him and leave, and boy was I wrong. We arrived at the party late and my friend's ex-boyfriend was there, we had become quite close. He introduced us to a few of their friends and before he left, he whispered in my ear "be careful". God was trying to warn me right then and there but obviously not trying to be a party pooper I went along with the ride and ignored the warnings. In short, the boy messed me up, he tried getting me drunk to sleep with him, then when I refused he pretended to understand but only to pass me on to his other friend, I found out he slept with two other girls that same evening, I felt disposable, cheap, like nothing and not as irreplaceable as I thought I was, or at least as my father told me. A week-long relationship was short but it left a stain. I lost all self-esteem, and even when I wanted to move on, I had lost all interest in boys. I turned dark, full emo, seeking darkness and lonely places, I was sad always, and listened to a lot of sad, angry music. Avoiding anything that reminded me of him and any other boy for that matter.

Like every drug, the high is temporary, and that excitement and joy of young love had ceased to exist. I kept my mind busy, reading novels and watching thriller movies. I was finally starting to find comfort in my loneliness. I had friends and family around always but when I was alone, the feelings would surface, feelings of loneliness, sadness, anger, and a feeling of being lost, but I was okay with it now, I had come to terms with that there would be no one to make me feel whole again.

The confusion that believing that a human can make us whole when in actual fact the One that we think is an addition to our life is the very core of wholeness. God is the source and foundation of life, we seek companionship and the one that never leaves.

Deuteronomy 31:8 "The LORD himself goes before you and will be with you; he will never leave you nor forsake you. Do not be afraid; do not be discouraged."

The One that will stay loyal and on our side is God, He is constant and consistent; He is the true definition of what love is.

Chapter Four- Misery loves Company

I stayed single for the rest of that year, but it didn't last long. The friend that warned me against his friend started pushing me closer to his older brother. We were all great friends; we worshipped together, drank, and partied together. We were very comfortable in this world, but though we claimed the glory and greatness of God, our hearts were not reflecting it.

I really didn't fall for this one, and not because he didn't have the looks or anything, he was a mixer of good and bad, everything was lovable and scary at the same time. For those wondering he was beautiful, slim in his figure and strong shoulders and a bold neck. I liked him, a lot, but just did not see him in that way.

We made good friends, and we related our misery, loss of a father, absent father, confused, and lost and misunderstood. We enjoyed the darkness we both carried, the loneliness and always feeling out of place. We were good as friends, bonding over the love of The Vampire Diaries, casting ourselves for roles, and finding pieces of ourselves in the darkness. We bonded over Adele and shared sad love lyrics; we were happy in our sadness; nothing could touch us when were united. We were great at making everyone around us happy, even each other but battled with our own hearts.

Somehow being around each other to share the sadness and misery, made the pain easier to bare or at least slightly forgettable.
With everyone around us telling us we would make a great couple, we started falling for it, You know how it goes, hearing the same thing over, and over again, you soon start to believe it. We didn't really act on anything; we were comfortable just the way we were.

9th December was his birthday; he invited us over for a party he was hosting at his house. When we arrived, we were welcomed by the family and friends that were present; I would introduce myself and get the sense that their reactions meant more than they were leading on.
I should've known better though, something always happens with these boys and their parties. Anyways found out we were dating, which was a shock to me, I did not accept it because even though I may have lowered my standards of receiving love, I was still old school, and taught how a lady carries herself. We ended up dating the following year when eventually asked me out, which didn't last very long; our relationship was brief and confused in the end.
He fell for someone else, someone he always wanted but never had the chance to be with before, so this time, he took the opportunity. Honestly found out in the most uneasy way but I wasn't hurt. The reason being, that I never really fell in love, I was bruised because it confirmed my insecurities. It was nothing new, just that I was never enough, or someone better is out there and would always replace me, and everything I knew and felt. I forgave him easily because though he left a scar, he was never mine, to

begin with, it was easy to move on from. It wasn't a visible scar, easy to hide and soon easy to forget.

The Lord reminded me that during my singleness, I prayed for a guy like him, I described him, I had specifics, and the Lord allowed room for him. He said even though I delivered him, doesn't mean he was the one I had planned for you, and even at a young age, details matter. The Lord is a God of order, ask and it shall be given, I left out a few things while praying and asking for him. And though I received him, He may not be handpicked and handed over by the Lord but God allowed it to happen, He allowed us to meet and for me to learn a lesson from it. "Amanda, you're not always the one." Harsh but true, because for a very long time, I believed I can make any guy happy, "they would be lucky to have me", I am their ultimate goal, only for God to humble me.

I had to carry this principle, not only with romantic relationships but with friendships as well. As people, we feed off each other and who we surround ourselves with on a daily basis is important. Who we share our thoughts, dreams, and secrets with, who we allow to advise us, pray with us, and for us, these people are very vital, not for the public to see but for the spirit man.

Proverbs 13: 20 says "Walk with the wise and become wise; associate with fools and get in trouble."

As I took time to evaluate my friendships and relationships in general, I was amazed still, to find that just because the relationship was found in a familiar place (church) didn't mean it was founded in Christ. God began to pick at every friend I have, whether they were feeding my purpose or delaying it.

Chapter Five- Mirror Mirror

Proverbs 27:17 As Iron sharpens iron, so a friend sharpens a friend.

Ever heard the saying "you are who you keep around". Meaning the people you keep around, whom you associate with, work or church, who you are in a romantic relationship with, represent you. There's another saying that says "show me your friends and I'll tell you who you are". There is always some sort of reflection happening or exchange between the two parties. All these influences have the capacity to effect change in your character and behavior.

I became who I was friends with, whoever I was around at that stage in my life, was how you would spot me, my character changed, the way I speak, the way I dress, who I like and don't like, everything was founded on who my friends were.

Most of my close friends were from church, all at different stages of my life. One was very popular, beautiful, the life of the party and I guess you could say trendy back then. She knew everyone and everyone knew her, and if they didn't know her they wanted to. Somehow, we became friends, but it came with so much pressure. The pressure of having to keep up, having to act like you know everything, or like everything they do, have things that are only at a certain standard. I have always been a simple person and some friendships stretched me to the point where I was unable to recognize myself. Self-esteem issues started to kick in, comparison started to build up.

Some friendships happened naturally, outside of the church, which was my first mistake. Don't get me wrong, it's okay to have friends outside of your church and belief, I have a few of those, but they understand that I am Christian first and that's the lifestyle I have chosen.

For a long time, I lost that conviction of why I was Christian and started to hide that part of me to fit in with the world, to be cooler, popular, more "fun" and less boring. I wanted to have fun and wild weekends that every young person experienced with their friends. Though my freedom was limited, because my mother did not play those games, I was still able to stretch myself to fit in the world and be Christian at the same time.

Some guy made an example of me in class once, as a "good balance" the girl that handles a wild night of partying and still is able to go to church on Sunday and pray. Granted I didn't drink alcohol, but that one took me by surprise. This guy was the same guy, who would ask me, where I would be during the weekend, wherever my friend and I were, was where the party was at.

Total shift, it completely took me by surprise, just a few years back I was the girl fully churchy, preached to people, used to get teased, and called "Pastor" and now I had become the gig guide. How transformation can take place bit by bit till you lose the entire image of who you are and it's just a memory.

Colossians 3:2"Set your mind on things above, not on things on the earth"

The proof is that when you choose yourself and please others daily, you become part of the world. As much as I believed and convinced myself that I'm thee Christian, my surroundings and people around me proved different. The scripture says "set your mind", meaning we need to choose and apply ourselves to heavenly things and things of God, and again choosing that over the tempting "fun" of the world. how you soon think is how you'll soon behave.

Chapter Six - Power of the Tongue

At some point m love for Hip-Hop switched from dance to music, listening to everything YMCMB, and that's still fire, just served me different back then. I had a song I ritually listened to on my way to and from school, I sang out the words with gusto, and somehow I believed it was made to build the confidence of young girls, or just females doing it for themselves.
The only issue was I kept singing the words out loud, calling myself those names, not knowing that I was actually planting an image that would later manifest.

Speaking things into existence is not faux or magic, it's real. If you say something to yourself or to things around you long enough and inconsistently, they will eventually come to fruition. The only issue was I did not expect this to come into reality as, it was "just lyrics to a song", just a line from a movie. It's the things we don't think are important that build.
I remember I was shocked when my Pastor said there is "no such thing as you were kidding". He said once it leaves your mouth, you have released creation, (mind-blowing, I know)
That alone is enough to make you take your words seriously. After all, we are creators on earth.

The words to the song, later reflected two years later, after the song was old and I had stopped listening to it. People at my new workplace started addressing me differently, no matter how hard I tried to be or show the real version of me, and people saw what I had planned and sown years ago.

If you're wondering what this song said, I'll give a little clue. : "I'm the baddest B####". Now that last word is a horrible word to refer a woman to, let alone yourself. I sang those lyrics, till people saw that. Now it can be very challenging when you are Christian, hardly go out and live in a strict household. All they thought of me was everything I was not.

I was told I'm adventurous and look like "fun", in which context I was scared to find out. I looked like the life of the party.

This all was completely the opposite of the girl that was there to earn to pay bills at home, go to church, and be in an honest relationship with her partner.

I started denying everything they said about me to myself because before I used to laugh it off, and laughing it off is not rejection but in fact a subtle acceptance of what is being said. I then boldly started saying "NO. I'm not that", "You got the wrong girl". Understanding very well that these are things they would never call me in front of an elder, I knew it was wrong to accept it as a Christian lady. I got into the position of what I wanted to be and how I wanted to be treated.

The bible has a lot of scriptures about what God says about and thinks about us, what He desires for us and how we should carry ourselves on earth. The issue is we are

more people pleasers than God pleasers.
My Bible says:
For we are God's handiwork, created in Christ Jesus to do good works, which God prepared in advance for us to do. (Eph 2; 10)
But you are a chosen people, a royal priesthood, a holy nation, God's special possession, that you may declare the praises of him who called you out of darkness into his wonderful light. (1 Pet 2:9)
I praise you because I am fearfully and wonderfully made; your works are wonderful, I know that full well (Psa 139:14)
These are only a few of many where we see what God is saying about us, and that it shouldn't matter what the world says, we define and find our identity in the One, the Creator of all, Our Father.
He loves me, He loves you, and He loves us more than we can ever love ourselves. So now I am careful what I say and sing to, what I allow to feed my spirit, either through visuals or sound.
It's the simplicity of planting, which is whatever seed you plant is what you will have. You plant oranges; you get more oranges, not apples.

Chapter Seven – Slow Poison

"Smart people know how to hold their tongue; their grandeur is to forgive and forget."
Proverbs 19:11 MSG

Normally we would rather "forgive" but never forget, just so we never get fooled again. But clearly, the Bible contradicts that idea. In pursuit of knowing yourself through the maker and being Christ-like, we might have to just let things go. Basically, forgiveness leaves us vulnerable to being disappointed and hurt again, it allows us to ignore the previous scars and allow trust and hopefully not being hurt again.

Godly principles on forgiveness fight every aspect of human behavior and feelings.

When forgiving someone, it's impossible to work from your feelings, I guess this is where Godly wisdom comes from. Jesus was betrayed by people that walked with Him, people that called Him the Messiah and then still chanted to kill him instead.

Instead of holding a grudge or waiting to punish them later, he prayed for them while on the cross, and he asked God to forgive them.

"Then Jesus said, "Father, forgive them, for they do not know what they do."

This has been the most trying part of my walk of faith with God, as I have spent time educating myself in the character of God and watching a forgiveness series, certain offenses and people started to pop into my mind.

And it was strange to think of some because I thought getting over it or moving on meant I forgave, but it meant that I had made peace with not making peace with someone. Though they are not aware of the anger and hurt I hold towards them, it's the person God is shaping me into that needs to let go of the past in order to evolve into who He has called me to be.

I think the toughest thing to ever forgive, is the offense that never receives an apology. I heard this quote once "Unforgiveness is like drinking poison and expecting the other person to die".

That really set with me, because I believed for a long time, that as long as I remember what they did to me and how they hurt me before, in other words, if I never forgave then they can never do me like that again. I was wrong, holding on to bitterness, hurts you more than it hurts them.

So I started the journey of forgiving one offense at a time. God knew I needed a guide or at least a road map, I started with writing down the names and every time I would turn to my journal, I would see the names and be reminded to forgive. Then I had to start with the least hurtful to forgive because you know there is a hierarchy to these things. Easy right forgave the lady that spoke to me like "she crazy" then had to erase her name.

Then it came to forgiving the big things, the big ones mean taking apart everything, stating the offense and how it made you feel.

What I noticed with this process was that the issue was not what was on the surface, the obvious, what we usually say, but it was the feelings, how it made you feel.

It is the feelings that build up the hurt and anger, granted some of these are a bit insane.

I then realized all the things I had to forgive happened around my teenage years, that family member that left after my father's passing, making me feel unwanted or abounded. Not enough to stay around for. It hurt and I carried that hurt for years, then I had to forgive.

Then the time I witnessed abuse between a family member and a partner. I hated that at the age of 15, I was exposed to what we usually hear about in the news or see on these thriller shows. The ordeal plays in my memory over and over, hearing the screams repeatedly. I must forgive.

Now the big hurrah, Back story: 17 years old, out and about, had been seeing this guy for like a week, was invited to this 18th birthday party, but the turned to a disaster, I was offered alcohol (I didn't drink alcohol) very strong alcohol, was then convinced to join him in a room "alone". Nothing happened, because I didn't drink nor was I stupid enough to lose my virginity to "some church boy". I mention that because it is the people we let our guards down for that sometimes, trip us off. I lost a bit of myself that night. I was never the same in the dating game. Was guarded, strong, lost trust for men in general? I lost hope in people, always expecting disappointment.

I'm walking this journey and willing to forgive, though I know if they were to walk into the room right now I would freeze I am trusting the process. I will forgive.

"If you forgive those who sin against you, your heavenly Father will forgive you."

Matthew 6:14 NLT

Notice how the last two offenses I said must and will forgive because it really doesn't happen overnight. It might take a week, a month, a year, or 4 years, but you will forgive.

Some are greater than others and some just seem too hard to forgive, but it will happen when the will is there.

Chapter Eight– The prodigal daughter

At some point in my life, I chose to rebel against what I knew. 16 years old church girl, mixed with the crowd she once envied. I want to experience life outside of the church, school, and home.

I wanted to "live a little "as they'd say. Explore outside of the norm, be with the free and live the life, or so I thought. There have been yearly church conferences happening around the same time this Hip-Hip event would take place. I had always wanted to but was never brave enough to do it and be well disobedient. Every sign not to go was there, our transport was late. We overspent on our budget including money to get home, when we managed to arrive at the event, we were able to forget the problems we would deal with.

This is the same as the prodigal son's story, *Luke 15:11-32*when he asked for and received his inheritance; he went around squandering it from a distant country. This is an important detail. He had to separate himself from his father's house and covering in order to do as he pleased. Sometimes we take ourselves out of a place of comfort, to find "freedom" not knowing the place we call home was never a prison and holding us hostage but was a safe place.

When the event ended, we found ourselves wondering where to go, in a minute, gunshots went off, and people scattered and ran everywhere. We were meant to be at one place but ended up at another. It is then that I did a silent prayer; we were stranded and a long way from home. Eventually, someone helped us out and we caught a lift with a group of people, this was a very eventful day, in short, we either would've been left on street lost and hungry, we would've been taken far away from home, shot or injured. So many instances.

It would be easy to say, "this is not a testimony, you should've just stayed home", but everyone, at some point in their lives has stepped out of God's covering. Whether it is in relationships or jobs etc. Dating someone you knew was not sent by God, having sex before marriage, we've all stepped out of his covering one way or another.

We woke up to find ourselves in a strange place. We passed home. Only to find out the people were from a different city altogether. We would have had even bigger problems than sleeping out.

I am certain God's sovereignty was at that place at that time. That though he saw us step out of His wing, He had compassion towards us.

"So he got up and went to his father. "But while he was still a long way off, his father saw him and was filled with compassion for him; he ran to his son, threw his arms around him, and kissed him."

Luke 15:20 NIV

I learned that the freedom we actually seek usually leaves us seeking more and needing validation from others. Please people and selves. It usually leaves us vulnerable and exposed to what the world had to offer and that's when the enemy can sneak in and distract you for good. As Christians, we have the Holy Spirit guiding us and our paths. Though it may seem like this life has too many rules and instructions. *Obedience is better than sacrifice (1 Samuel*

15:22)
"Because the Lord disciplines those he loves, as a father the son he delights in."
Proverbs 3:12 NIV

Chapter Nine- Full Circle

The journey I took in writing this book had me conflicted a lot on why would I be literally feeding people things to gossip about and judge me on. I had to pray long and hard about it and the answer returned in the simplest way. "This is not about you " I have shared stories about myself from the beginning but the point wasn't to just share them but to reveal the 2 most important facts God wanted us to know. One that He's always there, that Hos word, that He'll never leave us nor forsake us is true but sometimes we take longer to know that because we're fighting battles we shouldn't be in. That we make mistakes but He's in there with us and helps clean up the mess, aligning us back to His initial plan. The second point took me OUT!

On my way to work, He reminded me of the story of the three little pigs and the big bad wolf. Hang on it it gets good I promise. You know the story goes
The first pig uses straws to build his house, but the wolf huffs and puffs and blows the house down, the pig to the second pig's house which was made of sticks, and the wolf again huffed and puffed and blew it down, they then both ran to the third pig's house and that one was made of bricks. Wolf came again huffed and puffed but this time the house was secure the wolf couldn't take it down. This story was painting an image of our faith. Based on what we

are founded in and how we relate to God we could either be put in situations to let the enemy get to us or be armed and protected by the lord.

It also painted the image of the first pig being an unbeliever, the second pig being a believer but with no relationship with God, and the pig with the brick house, representing Christians that have a close relationship and fellowship with God.

The aim is not to gloat at the other pigs that our house is stronger and the choices they made were weak, or dumb but instead we build such a strong foundation and place that when they come running to us we don't judge them but welcome them with open arms.

So with that kindergarten memory let us walk and talk about the image of God that casts no judgments but fully loves and aim to bring glory to His Name

Chapter Ten- Free Indeed

For the longest time, I searched and searched for freedom, a way to express myself, a way I could find myself in this big world. Find the people I fit with and the types of things I like. I think everyone goes through some "soul searching" some time in our lives and the biggest issue is we search in every place but the right place.
Genesis 1: 26
Let us make man in our image, according to our likeness…
The bible already tells us who our creator is, and if we needed to know ourselves better, God would be the best place to search. Usually seeking identity means, we don't know who we are, so if we see the one who created us, and why He made us, we would soon learn to live according to that knowledge. Knowing who and whose we are the plans for our lives and purpose on earth.

Writing this brought a lot of anxiety but also relief, knowing that a lot can relate to searching for you in people or things, hoping for qualifications and positions in jobs, or with people to validate us. Seeking to belong and hopefully say "mama I made it". God proved to know me better than anyone ever could, and He proved to be present in all my walks and stumbles in life.
He protected me, guided me, covered and Loved me. Now when I go through life questions I can only hope that I

always go to Him first and not convince myself to hear His voice and please my feelings, but to do according to His will.

And I pray the same thing for you. That you may find restoration, healing, trust, patience, and the love you have been searching for. That the Almighty God may be so close to you that you hear Him speak. May He reveal His mysteries and plans to you, and may you grow closer and have a bond more potent than any bond, that when they search you, they find God first. May your life be a testimony always and may your Mind, Body, and Soul, honor and glorify God, all the days of your life. Amen

9 789356 109230

Printed by Libri Plureos GmbH in Hamburg, Germany